Top Cryptocurrencies You Should Know

A Deep Dive Into Bitcoin, Ethereum, Solana, Chainlink, and Other Powerful Digital Assets

By Joe Correa

Published by Live Stronger Faster

This book is for educational and informational purposes only. The author and publisher are not engaged in rendering legal, financial, or other professional advice. Readers should consult a qualified professional before making any financial decisions.

First Edition

Table of Contents

Introduction

Cryptocurrencies are no longer a fringe technology understood by only a handful of tech enthusiasts. They are shaping the future of finance, supply chains, gaming, decentralized applications, and even art. While there are over 20,000 cryptocurrencies in existence, only a handful are truly groundbreaking—offering real-world utility, long-term staying power, and serious investment potential.

In this book, we focus on the **top cryptocurrencies** you should understand, whether you're just starting out or already building a diversified crypto portfolio. This isn't just about buying the hottest coin of the month. It's about understanding **why** certain cryptocurrencies matter—what problems they solve, what makes them unique, and how they're likely to perform long term.

We'll begin with **Bitcoin**, the first and most dominant digital asset, which many call "digital gold." You'll learn how Bitcoin's limited supply, decentralized nature, and institutional adoption have made it the core of crypto investing. Next, we dive into **Ethereum**, the world's largest smart contract platform powering thousands of decentralized applications (dApps), DeFi protocols, and NFTs.

We'll also explore **emerging powerhouses** like **Solana**, known for its ultra-fast and low-cost transactions, and **Cardano**, which emphasizes academic research and scalability. Then we break down **Chainlink**, the oracle that brings real-world data to blockchains, enabling everything from DeFi pricing to sports-based prediction markets.

But we won't stop there. This book will also take you through other impactful projects such as **Polkadot** (for blockchain interoperability), **Avalanche** (for scalable DeFi), and **Polygon** (for Ethereum scaling). We'll cover real-world examples, use cases, pros and cons, and the long-term vision behind each one.

Whether you're building your first crypto wallet or looking to rebalance your portfolio with stronger long-term plays, this guide gives you the essential insights to make educated decisions. These are not meme coins or hype-based tokens. These are **infrastructure coins** and **mission-driven platforms** shaping the next internet.

By the end of this book, you'll walk away with a crystal-clear understanding of what each of these top cryptocurrencies does, why they matter, and how to evaluate their place in your personal investment strategy. This is your deep dive into the digital assets shaping tomorrow's economy.

Let's begin with the one that started it all—**Bitcoin**.

Chapter 1: Bitcoin — Digital Gold and the Future of Store of Value

Bitcoin, the first and most recognized cryptocurrency, revolutionized the concept of money. Introduced in 2009 by an anonymous figure known as *Satoshi Nakamoto*, Bitcoin was designed to offer a decentralized, peer-to-peer digital cash system free from government control and centralized banking. What sets Bitcoin apart is its fixed supply, decentralization, and strong security—all built on a blockchain that has never been hacked.

At its core, Bitcoin is a **digital store of value**. Just as gold has historically been used as a hedge against inflation and economic uncertainty, Bitcoin has earned the title "digital gold" due to its scarcity (limited to 21 million coins), divisibility, and portability. Unlike fiat currencies, which can be printed endlessly, Bitcoin's issuance is algorithmically controlled, reducing over time via halving events every four years. These events slash the amount of new BTC entering circulation, increasing scarcity and typically triggering bull markets.

Bitcoin operates on a **Proof-of-Work (PoW)** consensus mechanism, where miners solve complex mathematical problems to validate transactions and secure the network. This process ensures that transactions are immutable and irreversible. While critics argue that PoW consumes too much energy, proponents see it as a feature that strengthens Bitcoin's integrity by making attacks costly.

Adoption has skyrocketed in recent years. Large institutional investors, public companies like Tesla and MicroStrategy, and even countries like El Salvador have added Bitcoin to their balance sheets or legal frameworks. This shift from speculative asset to strategic reserve has legitimized Bitcoin in the eyes of the financial elite. Furthermore, Bitcoin is now available through ETFs, major trading platforms, and even retirement accounts, making it increasingly accessible to mainstream investors.

Bitcoin also acts as a lifeline in economically unstable countries. In places with hyperinflation, frozen bank accounts, or capital controls, citizens are turning to Bitcoin as a secure, censorship-resistant way to store and transfer value. Cross-border remittances using Bitcoin can bypass expensive fees and delays associated with traditional banking systems.

Despite its strengths, Bitcoin is not without limitations. It is relatively slow, with only seven transactions per second, and its scripting language is limited compared to platforms like Ethereum. That said, second-layer solutions such as the

Lightning Network have emerged to solve scalability issues by enabling instant, low-cost Bitcoin payments without sacrificing decentralization.

As Bitcoin evolves, it becomes more than just a currency—it becomes a financial operating system. Developers are now building applications directly on top of the Bitcoin blockchain or integrating it into financial platforms. Bitcoin's simplicity is its strength. It does one thing—store and transfer value—with unmatched reliability and decentralization.

For long-term investors, Bitcoin is seen as a core holding in any crypto portfolio. It has the longest track record, the strongest security, the largest network effect, and the clearest value proposition. While its price may fluctuate dramatically, its core fundamentals remain unchanged. Bitcoin is not just a trend; it's the foundation of the cryptocurrency revolution.

Bitcoin vs gold

Raj had just returned home from another grueling day working in finance. Despite the glossy office building and tailored suit, something never sat right with him. Every day he watched central banks flood the markets with more printed money, diluting the value of people's savings. As an analyst, he understood inflation, but it still frustrated him. His parents' retirement fund was shrinking in purchasing power, and the dollar he earned today was worth less tomorrow.

One night, he stumbled across a podcast episode titled *"What is Bitcoin?"* He hit play out of curiosity—and that decision changed everything.

The podcast host compared Bitcoin to gold, but better. It wasn't just scarce—it was mathematically finite. Only 21 million would ever exist. Unlike the government, no one could wake up and decide to "print" more. It was the first time Raj heard the phrase **"digital gold."** His ears perked up.

That weekend, Raj dove headfirst down the Bitcoin rabbit hole. He read the original whitepaper by Satoshi Nakamoto. He learned how miners validated transactions, how every block was recorded immutably on the blockchain, and how Bitcoin's codebase was open-source and available for anyone to inspect. He was mesmerized. It wasn't just about profit—it was about **freedom**. No gatekeepers. No intermediaries. No permission required.

Raj bought his first $100 worth of Bitcoin when the price was $6,000. It wasn't much, but it was symbolic. Over the next few months, he watched it climb to $10,000, then $20,000. He felt like he was part of a revolution. But with the highs came the lows. The market corrected sharply. Bitcoin dropped. Friends mocked him. His parents warned him it was a bubble. But Raj didn't flinch.

He started attending local Bitcoin meetups in the city. There he met software developers, entrepreneurs, and even retirees—all drawn by the same spark: the idea that money could be sovereign again. One of the regulars, an old Austrian economist named Henry, told him, "I see in Bitcoin the same store-of-value properties we had in gold—except now it's portable, divisible, and programmable."

The turning point came when Raj visited Venezuela to help a nonprofit organization. The local currency was nearly worthless. Supermarket shelves were empty, and people were desperate. But then he saw something remarkable—locals using Bitcoin through mobile apps to buy food and medicine. Even in one of the harshest economic conditions, Bitcoin was working.

He realized Bitcoin wasn't just an investment. It was hope. A lifeline for those trapped by corruption and inflation. It was the first time he saw the phrase **"banking the unbanked"** in action.

Raj went all in. He created a blog, wrote beginner guides, and started consulting for businesses accepting Bitcoin payments. His audience grew. He was invited to speak at conferences and became known as a Bitcoin educator. He diversified his holdings, but Bitcoin remained his largest position.

Years later, when Bitcoin surpassed $100,000, Raj didn't sell. For him, Bitcoin wasn't just about wealth—it was about **values**. It was about building a parallel financial system, one that couldn't be manipulated by politics or privilege.

He looked at his digital wallet, seeing those first few sats from years ago still sitting there—untouched but life-changing. Bitcoin had become more than code. It had become a philosophy. A revolution. And for Raj, it all started with a late-night podcast and a decision to question the system.

Chapter 2: Ethereum — The World Computer and Smart Contract Pioneer

Ethereum is much more than just another cryptocurrency. While Bitcoin revolutionized the idea of decentralized money, Ethereum introduced something far more powerful: **programmable blockchain applications.** Often referred to as the "world computer," Ethereum enables developers to build decentralized applications (dApps), smart contracts, and entire digital economies directly on its blockchain.

Launched in 2015 by **Vitalik Buterin** and a group of visionary developers, Ethereum emerged as a platform that solved Bitcoin's most significant limitation—lack of programmability. Whereas Bitcoin was designed as a secure and simple store of value, Ethereum was built to be an open-source ecosystem where code could execute automatically without human interference. This brought forth **smart contracts**, which are self-executing programs that run when specific conditions are met. Think of them like legal agreements—but coded, transparent, and unchangeable once deployed.

Smart contracts power everything on Ethereum—from decentralized finance (DeFi) protocols and NFTs to games, identity systems, and DAOs (Decentralized Autonomous

Organizations). Ethereum essentially acts as the backbone of **Web3**—a decentralized internet where ownership and value are embedded directly into the code. For example, instead of trusting a bank, a smart contract can lend you funds, hold collateral, and enforce repayment, all without a middleman.

One of the most critical aspects of Ethereum is its vast **developer community**, the largest in crypto. This network of programmers constantly contributes to the ecosystem, building new use cases and improving the core protocol. Ethereum is also responsible for launching some of the most influential crypto projects, such as Uniswap, Aave, Compound, and OpenSea. The explosion of decentralized applications has made Ethereum the center of a trillion-dollar digital economy.

Originally launched with a Proof-of-Work (PoW) consensus model like Bitcoin, Ethereum made a historic transition to **Proof-of-Stake (PoS)** in 2022 through a major upgrade known as *The Merge*. This upgrade drastically reduced Ethereum's energy usage by over 99% and opened the door to future scalability enhancements, such as **sharding**. Ethereum's roadmap focuses on increasing transaction throughput, reducing fees, and supporting mass adoption without compromising security or decentralization.

Gas fees—essentially transaction costs—have been one of

Ethereum's main pain points. During periods of high demand, these fees can become extremely expensive. However, the ecosystem has responded with **Layer 2 solutions** like Arbitrum, Optimism, and zkSync. These scaling technologies help take load off the main chain, allowing users to transact faster and cheaper without losing the security of Ethereum's base layer.

ETH, the native token of Ethereum, plays several roles. It's used to pay for gas fees, secure the network through staking, and act as collateral in many DeFi applications. Unlike Bitcoin, which is primarily a store of value, ETH is a **utility token**—fueling the very functions that make Ethereum work. And with EIP-1559 (a major protocol update), a portion of every transaction fee is now burned, making ETH **deflationary** over time.

Ethereum is far from just a speculative asset. It's a **platform for innovation**. It's where new economies are born, where artists can tokenize their work, where banks are being replaced with code, and where identity, privacy, and ownership are being redefined for the digital age.

Whether you're a builder, investor, or curious learner, understanding Ethereum is non-negotiable. It is the foundation of most of what exists in crypto beyond Bitcoin, and its growth potential is vast. As regulations evolve and traditional industries explore tokenization and blockchain integration, Ethereum is well-positioned to be at the center of it all.

Amara the digital artist

Amara was a digital artist based in Lagos, Nigeria. For years, she struggled to monetize her work. Online galleries took hefty commissions, local buyers were scarce, and her art was often plagiarized without recourse. Then one day, while browsing Reddit, she discovered something called an **NFT**—a non-fungible token—built on the Ethereum blockchain. She was skeptical at first, but curious enough to dig deeper.

As she read more, she learned about Ethereum—not just as a currency, but as an open-source platform for building applications that lived on the blockchain. The idea of a **decentralized internet** fascinated her. No gatekeepers. No approval processes. No limits. Ethereum wasn't just a coin—it was a global computer, and smart contracts were the apps.

She downloaded a crypto wallet and minted her first NFT on an Ethereum-based platform. Within a week, she sold it to a buyer in Germany for 0.2 ETH—more than she'd made from an entire local exhibition. That moment was electric.

Ethereum had opened a new world where her art could live digitally, verifiably, and profitably.

But it didn't stop there.

Amara got invited to a virtual artist DAO, a decentralized community of creators funding each other's projects. The smart contract that governed their treasury couldn't be edited or corrupted. Proposals were submitted and voted on by members using governance tokens. She marveled at how **trustless** and transparent it all was. No one controlled it, yet it worked flawlessly.

One day, she stumbled into DeFi—decentralized finance. Using just her phone, Amara swapped ETH for stablecoins on Uniswap, lent those stablecoins on Aave, and earned passive interest without involving a single bank. She wasn't just making art anymore; she was becoming financially independent through code.

Gas fees, though, were a pain. Minting her second collection during a high-demand week cost her over $100 in fees. She learned about **Layer 2 solutions** and moved some of her work to Arbitrum and Polygon, scaling her operations with lower fees and faster transactions. She felt like she was coding her own financial system—no banker required.

As Ethereum upgraded to Proof-of-Stake, Amara noticed the environmental shift. Her community had long criticized crypto's energy usage. But with The Merge, Ethereum's carbon footprint plummeted. It gave her pride to be part of something evolving—ethically and technically.

Years passed, and Amara wasn't just an artist anymore. She became a builder. She took courses in Solidity, the Ethereum programming language. She created a dApp that allowed emerging artists in developing countries to mint NFTs for free on Layer 2 networks. Her dApp won a global hackathon. She didn't need a degree. She didn't need Silicon Valley. She just needed the Ethereum blockchain and her will to learn.

One evening, as she sat on her balcony overlooking the city, she opened her wallet. She saw ETH, governance tokens, NFTs, and yield-bearing assets—all earned by participating in a global, permissionless ecosystem. She smiled. Ethereum had done more than change her finances. It had changed her identity. From outsider to creator. From struggling artist to tech pioneer.

And it all began with a question: *What is Ethereum?*

Chapter 3: Solana — High-Speed Blockchain for the Next Generation of Apps

Solana is one of the fastest and most scalable blockchains in the world, earning a reputation as the go-to platform for high-performance decentralized applications (dApps), especially in gaming, NFTs, and DeFi. While Bitcoin and Ethereum laid the groundwork for decentralization, Solana reimagined blockchain architecture with one goal in mind: **speed without sacrificing low cost**.

Launched in 2020 by **Anatoly Yakovenko**, a former Qualcomm engineer, Solana introduced a novel hybrid consensus mechanism that combines **Proof of History (PoH)** and **Proof of Stake (PoS)**. Proof of History is a cryptographic clock that timestamps transactions before they enter the ledger, which significantly reduces confirmation time and allows the network to process **65,000+ transactions per second**—all while maintaining low fees averaging just fractions of a cent.

This level of performance makes Solana attractive for applications that require real-time responsiveness, such as **decentralized exchanges**, **blockchain gaming**, **NFT**

marketplaces, and **micropayments**. It also allows developers to build applications that simply aren't practical on slower, more expensive chains like Ethereum without scaling layers.

Solana's ecosystem grew rapidly due to this scalability advantage. Projects like **Magic Eden** (NFT marketplace), **Stepn** (move-to-earn fitness app), and **Serum** (decentralized exchange) have all contributed to Solana's surge in popularity. Solana's integration with **Metaplex**, a protocol for minting and managing NFTs, made it one of the most active NFT platforms during the boom.

Despite its strengths, Solana has experienced growing pains. The network has suffered from **downtime incidents**, where transaction throughput overwhelmed the system, causing temporary outages. Critics argue this compromises decentralization and resilience. However, Solana Labs continues to address these issues through upgrades and validator network expansions.

Solana also shines in **developer accessibility**. Unlike Ethereum, which requires learning Solidity, Solana developers use **Rust, C, or C++**, which opens the door to a broader pool of programmers. Its strong documentation, grant programs, and hackathons have helped attract thousands of developers to its ecosystem.

The native token **SOL** plays a critical role. It's used to pay for transactions, participate in governance proposals, and stake for securing the network. SOL has also been used as collateral in various lending protocols and liquidity pools, allowing users to earn passive rewards. As usage increases, demand for SOL grows, creating a positive feedback loop for the token's value.

Solana is also a frontrunner in **Web3 mobile integration**. In 2022, the Solana team announced **Solana Mobile** and its flagship phone, the *Saga*, built to make crypto-native mobile applications more accessible. This effort reflects a growing belief that the next wave of blockchain users will interact primarily via smartphones.

Solana's long-term vision focuses on **mainstream adoption**. With lightning-fast speeds, negligible fees, and active development, it has a legitimate shot at onboarding the next billion users into blockchain. However, it must continue improving network reliability and decentralization to maintain trust.

In a world increasingly driven by real-time data, gaming, social media, and digital ownership, Solana offers a powerful infrastructure that's ready to meet these demands today—not in five years. For investors and developers alike, understanding Solana's architecture, community, and trajectory is crucial when evaluating next-gen blockchain opportunities.

The story of Michael and Solana

Miguel was a game developer based in São Paulo, obsessed with two things: creating immersive online worlds and eliminating friction between players and rewards. He'd built browser games since his teenage years, but something always held him back—latency, payment barriers, and greedy app stores taking cuts of his in-game economies. When he discovered blockchain gaming, it felt like a breath of fresh air. But it wasn't until he stumbled upon **Solana** that everything clicked.

The first time he deployed a mini play-to-earn game on Ethereum, he was thrilled... until users complained. "Why do I need to pay $70 just to mint a sword?" one player asked. Gas fees were killing the experience. Miguel was frustrated. His vision of real-time, decentralized gameplay felt out of reach. That's when another developer in a Discord server recommended Solana.

"Try Solana," they said. "It's like Ethereum on turbo. Near-zero fees. Real-time speed."

Skeptical but desperate, Miguel started learning Rust and began building on the Solana blockchain. The difference was night and day. He could now process thousands of in-game transactions without his players paying anything more than a fraction of a cent. He built a full RPG where characters leveled up, collected items, and even bought land—all secured on-chain, with no lags or delays.

Word spread fast. His game, *Eternum Quest*, gained thousands of users within weeks. A player from the Philippines wrote him: "Your game helped me pay for my sister's medical bills." Miguel was stunned. Blockchain gaming wasn't just fun—it was empowering people.

He minted his own in-game NFTs using **Metaplex** and sold them on **Magic Eden**, Solana's most popular NFT marketplace. Items sold like wildfire—glowing swords, rare armor, mythical mounts—all secured by smart contracts and tradable between players globally. The game took on a life of its own. Communities formed. Guilds launched. And Miguel, the solo dev, suddenly found himself leading a movement.

But not everything was perfect.

One weekend, Solana went down. The network halted due to a spam attack that overwhelmed transaction capacity. His users panicked. Some accused him of building on an unreliable chain. Miguel felt defeated. But then, Solana Labs rolled out updates, and validator communities worked around the clock to increase stability. He realized this was still a frontier—messy, chaotic, but full of potential.

He kept building.

Solana's **mobile-first strategy** fascinated him. When they released the *Saga* phone, designed specifically for Web3, Miguel started thinking beyond desktop games. He launched a mobile companion app that synced with his main game, and thanks to Solana's lightning speed, players could earn and trade tokens instantly from anywhere. He was living his dream—building a cross-platform game where rewards were real, assets were owned, and players were the economy.

One night, after a global tournament inside *Eternum Quest*, Miguel watched as 10,000 simultaneous users bought potions, traded gear, and earned tokens—all without a single complaint about fees or speed. He leaned back in his chair, grinning. Solana wasn't just a blockchain. It was **infrastructure**—the kind that made dreams like his possible.

For Miguel, Solana wasn't a speculative coin. It was a **canvas**. A fast, flexible, affordable digital playground where builders like him could rewrite the rules of ownership, commerce, and fun.

Chapter 4: Chainlink – The Oracle That Connects Blockchains to the Real World

While blockchains like Bitcoin and Ethereum have revolutionized digital trust, they have one major limitation: they can't access real-world data on their own. Blockchains are **closed systems**, meaning they can verify what happens on-chain but are blind to external events like stock prices, weather conditions, or sports scores. This limitation severely restricts the potential of smart contracts—unless they can connect to external data in a secure and reliable way.

That's where **Chainlink** comes in. Chainlink is a decentralized **oracle network** that acts as a bridge between the blockchain world and the outside world. It allows smart contracts to securely access off-chain data, APIs, events, and even other blockchains. Without a reliable oracle like Chainlink, smart contracts would be isolated—unable to interact with dynamic, real-time information.

Launched in 2017 by **Sergey Nazarov** and **Steve Ellis**, Chainlink quickly became the leading oracle solution in the crypto space. Its native token, **LINK**, is used to pay node operators for retrieving data, performing computations, and ensuring uptime. Chainlink is now deeply integrated into major DeFi protocols, insurance products, NFT projects, and even traditional financial systems exploring tokenization.

The **importance of oracles** cannot be overstated. Take decentralized finance (DeFi) for example. A lending protocol needs real-time price data to determine when to liquidate undercollateralized loans. If the price feed is wrong, users could get unfairly liquidated—or the protocol could go bankrupt. Chainlink solves this with decentralized data feeds called **Chainlink Price Feeds**, which aggregate data from multiple sources and nodes to prevent manipulation or single points of failure.

Chainlink doesn't rely on one oracle—it uses **multiple independent nodes** and **data sources** to verify truth and accuracy. This is what sets it apart from centralized oracles, which can be hacked, manipulated, or simply go offline. With Chainlink, smart contracts can access data with **high integrity, redundancy, and uptime**.

But Chainlink is much more than just price data. Its capabilities include **Verifiable Randomness (VRF)**—used in gaming and NFTs to generate provably fair outcomes; **Proof of Reserve**—used to verify that real-world assets like tokenized gold or fiat-backed stablecoins are actually backed by reserves; and **Cross-Chain Interoperability Protocol**

(CCIP)—a breakthrough that allows secure messaging and data sharing across different blockchains.

In 2023, Chainlink launched **Chainlink Functions**, enabling developers to call any web API within a smart contract—greatly expanding dApp capabilities. This makes it possible to create hybrid smart contracts that use on-chain code and off-chain data in a seamless, secure flow. For example, a smart contract could verify your real-world credit score before issuing a blockchain loan.

Chainlink's real-world adoption is expanding rapidly. It's been used by **Google Cloud**, **SWIFT**, and **AccuWeather**, showing its enterprise-grade potential. Governments, financial institutions, and global corporations are increasingly integrating Chainlink oracles as they explore blockchain-based infrastructure.

For token holders, the LINK token is essential to the system. It's staked by node operators to ensure good behavior, slashed in case of misreporting, and used as a reward for providing quality data. With the launch of **Chainlink Staking v0.1 and v0.2**, the network took its first major steps toward **economic security** via community-based validation.

Chainlink isn't flashy. It doesn't attract hype like meme coins or NFTs. But it is **foundational**—a core infrastructure layer that quietly enables the most powerful innovations in Web3. Without oracles, smart contracts are like smartphones with no internet. With Chainlink, they become limitless.

For builders, investors, and institutions alike, Chainlink represents a major leap toward real-world blockchain adoption. It's the connective tissue that will allow blockchains to interact with traditional systems—and with the real world—safely, securely, and at scale.

Leah's aha moment

Leah was a data scientist working at a major insurance firm in London. She had built her career around numbers—risk models, actuarial tables, claims automation. But as the digital world evolved, she saw a growing disconnect between traditional systems and the promise of smart contracts. Blockchain fascinated her, yet something always felt incomplete.

She understood the potential: autonomous code replacing red tape, instant claims payouts, self-executing agreements. But one question nagged her constantly: *How do these contracts know what's real?* How could a smart contract know when a flood occurred, or a flight was delayed, or a commodity's price changed?

Her answer came during a blockchain conference in Amsterdam. A speaker presented a protocol called **Chainlink**—described as an "oracle network" that allows blockchains to connect to real-world data. It was like plugging the outside world into the blockchain. Weather, sports, finance, APIs—Chainlink could feed all of it into smart contracts in a way that was decentralized, tamper-proof, and secure.

Leah was hooked.

She returned to London and immediately began experimenting. Her firm had been toying with blockchain-based microinsurance policies for farmers in Southeast Asia—policies that would automatically pay out if drought conditions lasted beyond 21 days. But the problem had always been: *who decides when a drought actually happened?* If the system was centralized, it could be manipulated. If decentralized, it couldn't access weather data.

Chainlink solved both problems.

Using **Chainlink oracles**, Leah built a pilot that connected local weather APIs directly to smart contracts. She used **Chainlink VRF** (Verifiable Random Function) for fair risk distribution among policyholders and insurers. She implemented **Proof of Reserve** to verify that tokenized insurance pools were fully backed. Her project went from theory to prototype in under a month.

When she demoed it to the executive board, the reaction was stunned silence. Then applause.

They greenlit a pilot in Indonesia. For the first time, farmers would receive instant payouts the moment drought thresholds were met—no paperwork, no fraud, no bureaucracy. Just code and data, verified by Chainlink.

But Leah didn't stop there.

She joined online developer forums, where she connected with Chainlink node operators from around the world—people who ran decentralized data feeds and staked **LINK** tokens to secure the network. She learned how LINK was used as collateral, how it incentivized accurate data reporting, and how Chainlink's economic model ensured long-term integrity.

She even watched **Chainlink Staking v0.1** launch and joined the waitlist for v0.2. She wasn't just building with Chainlink—she was helping secure it.

Months later, she spoke at the same Amsterdam conference where she'd first heard of Chainlink. Her topic: *"Decentralized Oracles in Real-World Risk Management."* Her use case became a flagship example of how blockchain could impact billions—not just traders in crypto, but farmers, workers, and everyday people in underserved markets.

After her talk, a young developer from Brazil approached her. "I loved your speech," he said. "But what happens if Chainlink disappears?"

She smiled. "That's the beauty of it. Chainlink isn't a company. It's a **network**—one that anyone can run, use, or build on. It's not going anywhere."

Later that night, as she scrolled through data feeds from her pilot project, she realized something profound: Chainlink wasn't just feeding data into contracts. It was **feeding trust** into systems that had long failed people.

It was the invisible bridge between reality and code—turning smart contracts from digital toys into real-world tools.

Chapter 5: Cardano — Academic Blockchain for a Sustainable and Scalable Future

Cardano is one of the most rigorously researched and academically grounded blockchain platforms in existence. Founded in 2017 by **Charles Hoskinson**, one of the co-founders of Ethereum, Cardano was built from the ground up to solve the blockchain trilemma: scalability, decentralization, and security—all while remaining environmentally sustainable and verifiable through formal academic methods.

Unlike most blockchain projects, Cardano is built using **peer-reviewed research** and **formal methods**, meaning every component of its design is based on academic papers and mathematically provable code. This academic rigor is part of what makes Cardano unique and attractive to institutions, developers, and governments seeking long-term, stable blockchain infrastructure.

The platform operates in multiple layers. The **Cardano Settlement Layer (CSL)** handles value transfers, while the **Cardano Computation Layer (CCL)** manages smart contracts and decentralized applications. This separation allows for flexibility, easier upgrades, and modular development. It also helps keep the core blockchain lightweight and secure.

Cardano uses a **Proof-of-Stake (PoS)** consensus mechanism called **Ouroboros**, which is one of the first provably secure PoS protocols, validated by academic peer review. Unlike Proof-of-Work systems like Bitcoin, Ouroboros is energy-efficient and scalable. Stakeholders participate by delegating their ADA tokens to **stake pools**, earning rewards while helping to secure the network. This system encourages decentralization by giving smaller players a chance to earn yields without needing expensive mining equipment.

The native token, **ADA**, is used for staking, paying transaction fees, and participating in governance. ADA is named after **Ada Lovelace**, a 19th-century mathematician often regarded as the world's first computer programmer. Cardano's commitment to education and global access is evident even in its branding.

Cardano's smart contract functionality was introduced through the **Alonzo upgrade** in 2021, enabling the deployment of decentralized applications (dApps). Since then, developers have launched DeFi platforms, NFT marketplaces, and DAOs on the Cardano network, although adoption has been slower compared to Ethereum or Solana due to more complex development tooling and delayed feature rollouts.

One of Cardano's defining principles is its **focus on real-world use cases** in developing countries. Through its parent company **Input Output Global (IOG)**, Cardano has partnered with governments and NGOs across Africa and Latin America to implement blockchain-based solutions in education, healthcare, and identity verification. For example, it partnered with the Ethiopian Ministry of Education to develop a blockchain system for verifying student credentials across five million users.

Cardano also emphasizes **sustainability**. It has one of the lowest energy footprints among major blockchains. Its long-term strategy includes **Voltaire**, a governance system that allows ADA holders to vote on network proposals and project funding. This model aims to transform Cardano into a **self-governed ecosystem**, where development decisions are decentralized and community-driven.

The **Hydra scaling solution** is another major innovation. It's a Layer 2 protocol that enables fast and cheap microtransactions by creating off-chain channels, significantly improving throughput without compromising security. Hydra will be key to Cardano's goal of handling global-scale financial applications and smart contract execution.

Cardano has faced criticism for being slow to ship features compared to competitors, but this is largely due to its scientific approach to development. Every update goes through rigorous testing and review. While this may frustrate fast-moving investors, it builds a foundation for long-term reliability.

In summary, Cardano represents a thoughtful, research-driven approach to blockchain. It's not about hype or quick wins. It's about creating a sustainable, scalable, and inclusive system that can serve millions of users across the globe with minimal environmental impact. For those who value vision, academic integrity, and a long-term roadmap, Cardano is one of the most important projects in the cryptocurrency space.

Amira's blockchain story

Amira was a high school teacher in Nairobi with a passion for education and technology. Every day, she taught her students math and science with limited resources—broken chalkboards, aging textbooks, and no computers. Yet she believed deeply in the future. Her dream was simple: to give every student a digital identity that couldn't be lost, stolen, or forged.

She had heard whispers of blockchain, mostly in the context of Bitcoin and speculation. But one day, at a community tech event, she saw a presentation that captured her imagination. The speaker introduced a project called **Cardano**, explaining how it had partnered with the Ethiopian government to create **blockchain-based student IDs** that could track academic performance securely from grade school to university.

Amira was stunned. It wasn't just a tech buzzword. It was a solution to real problems. In her own school, records were often lost when students moved or when floods damaged paperwork. Fraudulent degrees were also a major issue in the region. The idea that students could **own their academic records** on an unchangeable, accessible platform was revolutionary.

That evening, she researched Cardano obsessively. She learned about its founder, **Charles Hoskinson**, and how Cardano was built on **peer-reviewed science**. Unlike the fast-moving crypto projects filled with hype, Cardano moved slowly—deliberately—prioritizing security and long-term sustainability.

She read about **Ouroboros**, the energy-efficient Proof-of-Stake protocol that secured the Cardano network, and how anyone could delegate their **ADA tokens** to earn rewards. It was inclusive and fair, unlike traditional systems where the wealthy always had the advantage.

Inspired, Amira joined a developer training program supported by **Input Output Global**, the research company behind Cardano. She learned how to write smart contracts and how Cardano used **Plutus**, a secure programming language built on Haskell. It wasn't easy, but it made sense—clean, logical, and safe.

She built her first decentralized application: a simple tool that allowed students to upload and verify school certificates. The data was stored immutably. Teachers could sign off on progress reports, and employers could later verify their authenticity with a single click.

The pilot spread quickly.

Other schools in her district adopted it. Universities took notice. And soon, Amira was leading a grassroots movement for educational reform powered by blockchain. With help from a global Cardano community, she began integrating **identity tools**, scholarship tracking, and even **micro-scholarships** funded through decentralized finance on the Cardano network.

She watched proudly as students who had never seen a computer used mobile phones to access their digital transcripts and verify scholarship eligibility. One student told her, "For the first time, I feel like the system sees me."

Amira's project gained traction. She was invited to speak at conferences, sharing how **Cardano wasn't just a cryptocurrency—it was an ecosystem for real-world change**. She spoke about sustainability, identity, and the right to education. And people listened.

When **Hydra**, Cardano's Layer 2 scaling solution, launched, Amira was ready. Her app scaled easily, handling more schools and students than ever. The fees were low, the speed was high, and the reliability was unmatched.

She kept her ADA in a staking pool that funded development grants for African projects. Every block produced meant more educational apps, more progress, more independence.

One evening, sitting under the Nairobi sky, she looked through the dashboard of her app—thousands of students, each one represented by a line of code and a dream. Verified. Immutable. Belonging to them alone.

Cardano, she thought, wasn't fast or flashy. But it was **honest, intentional, and built to last**.

Chapter 6: Polkadot — Interoperability and the Multi-Chain Future

In the rapidly growing world of blockchain, one of the biggest limitations is **interoperability**. Most blockchains operate in silos. Bitcoin doesn't talk to Ethereum. Ethereum doesn't talk to Solana. This fragmentation limits the ability of decentralized applications (dApps) to share data and assets across chains. That's the exact problem **Polkadot** set out to solve—and why it's considered one of the most ambitious and innovative blockchain projects in existence.

Polkadot was created by **Dr. Gavin Wood**, another co-founder of Ethereum and the creator of its programming language, Solidity. Launched in 2020, Polkadot is designed as a **Layer 0** protocol—meaning it's a foundational blockchain that connects other blockchains. It provides the infrastructure for a decentralized internet where multiple chains, or "parachains," can communicate and exchange data securely and efficiently.

At the heart of Polkadot is the **Relay Chain**, its central chain responsible for security and coordination. Around it are the **parachains**, independent blockchains that plug into the Relay Chain. Each parachain can have its own token, rules, and logic, but benefit from the shared security and interoperability Polkadot provides.

What makes Polkadot truly unique is its **shared security model**. Parachains don't need to build their own validator networks or spend excessive resources securing themselves—they "borrow" security from the Relay Chain. This creates a highly scalable, secure environment where developers can launch optimized blockchains for specific use cases without starting from scratch.

To connect to the Polkadot network as a parachain, projects must win a **slot auction**, which involves staking large amounts of DOT (Polkadot's native token) for a set period. These auctions encourage long-term commitment and community involvement, as users often contribute DOT to help their favorite projects win slots—earning rewards in return. This model has already launched dozens of successful parachains in areas like DeFi, identity, gaming, and data privacy.

DOT is the utility and governance token of the Polkadot ecosystem. It serves several purposes: staking to secure the network, bonding to connect new parachains, and voting on governance proposals. Polkadot uses **Nominated Proof of**

Stake (NPoS), where nominators back validators they trust, promoting decentralization while maintaining strong security.

Polkadot is also known for its powerful governance framework. Unlike many other blockchains, Polkadot has a built-in system for **on-chain governance**, allowing stakeholders to vote on upgrades and protocol changes. This eliminates the need for hard forks and enables smoother, community-driven evolution.

On the developer side, Polkadot is built using **Substrate**, a modular blockchain framework that allows developers to create custom blockchains easily and plug them into the Polkadot ecosystem. This drastically lowers the barrier to entry for launching new, application-specific chains that are interoperable from day one.

The Polkadot ecosystem is growing rapidly, with parachains like **Acala (DeFi hub), Moonbeam (Ethereum compatibility), Astar (dApp platform), and Phala (privacy)** gaining traction. Each of these projects leverages the cross-chain features of Polkadot to build services that interact with multiple blockchains in real time.

Polkadot also has a "cousin" blockchain called **Kusama**, known as its "canary network." Kusama acts as a live testing ground for Polkadot upgrades, allowing developers to experiment and deploy innovations quickly before rolling them out to the main Polkadot chain. This two-tier system accelerates innovation while maintaining security on the mainnet.

In summary, Polkadot is not just another blockchain—it's a **blockchain of blockchains**. It aims to unify the fragmented crypto ecosystem by enabling secure cross-chain communication. As blockchain adoption grows, the ability to connect and scale across multiple networks will be crucial. Polkadot is betting that the future isn't one chain to rule them all—but many chains, working together.

Dominic, the developer

Dominic was a blockchain developer who couldn't sit still. Every time a new chain launched, he wanted to explore it. Ethereum, Solana, Avalanche—he had dabbled in them all. But the deeper he went, the more frustrated he became. Each chain had different rules, incompatible wallets, separate tokens, and no easy way to connect projects or data. It was like building apps on islands with no bridges.

He dreamed of a unified blockchain universe, where smart contracts could speak to each other, where assets could move freely, and where innovation didn't require starting from zero every time.

That's when he discovered **Polkadot**.

He first heard the name in a podcast. "Polkadot is building the internet of blockchains," the host said. That one phrase grabbed him. He stayed up all night reading the whitepaper by **Dr. Gavin Wood**, the same man who helped build Ethereum. The more he read, the more excited he became.

Polkadot wasn't just a new chain—it was a **Layer 0 protocol**, a platform designed to connect other blockchains called **parachains**. They'd all plug into a central Relay Chain for security and coordination. It was like a digital nervous system where different limbs could move independently but still work in harmony.

Dominic joined the Polkadot developer community and started learning **Substrate**, Polkadot's modular framework for building parachains. Within weeks, he was coding his own chain from scratch—something he'd never thought possible. He didn't need to worry about validators or security; the Relay Chain handled that. He could focus on what mattered: features, user experience, and functionality.

He built **CrossWorld**, a cross-chain NFT platform that let users mint an NFT on one parachain and trade it on another. An artist on Astar could sell to a buyer on Moonbeam without ever leaving their own ecosystem. It felt like the beginning of the internet all over again—but decentralized and community-owned.

To launch his parachain, Dominic needed to win a **slot auction**. He didn't have enough DOT tokens on his own, so he launched a **crowdloan campaign**, inviting supporters to stake their DOT in exchange for early access and reward tokens. The campaign went viral. Hundreds of users backed him, believing in his vision of a connected NFT economy. They won the slot.

CrossWorld went live.

In its first month, artists from four continents used it to mint and sell NFTs. Developers from other parachains began integrating it, and Dominic was blown away by the collaborative energy. Polkadot wasn't competitive—it was **complementary**. Everyone was building pieces of a shared future.

But the best moment came when a small game studio from Chile messaged him. They had built an RPG game on Kusama and wanted to plug into CrossWorld. Kusama, Polkadot's canary network, let developers test and deploy faster. Dominic agreed. They linked chains using **XCMP (Cross-Chain Message Passing)**—Polkadot's protocol for secure chain-to-chain communication.

And it worked. Flawlessly.

Players could earn NFT rewards in the game and trade them on CrossWorld instantly. No bridges. No wrappers. Just clean, seamless interoperability. For Dominic, it felt like magic.

Over time, he became a thought leader in the Polkadot space, speaking at events, writing tutorials, and helping new developers enter the ecosystem. He staked his DOT, voted on governance proposals, and even contributed to runtime upgrades. Polkadot wasn't just his platform—it was his **digital nation**.

One night, as he watched parachains syncing like stars orbiting a cosmic core, he felt a sense of peace. This wasn't just about blockchains. It was about unity. About giving power back to builders. About enabling a world where **freedom and collaboration** replaced silos and scarcity.

Polkadot didn't want to be the only chain. It wanted to be **the glue** that held them all together.

And Dominic knew, without a doubt, that this was the future.

Chapter 7: Avalanche — High-Speed DeFi and Enterprise-Ready Blockchain

Avalanche is a high-performance blockchain platform designed to combine the best of scalability, speed, and decentralization without sacrificing security. Launched in 2020 by **Ava Labs**, Avalanche has quickly become one of the most respected and widely adopted platforms in the cryptocurrency space—particularly among decentralized finance (DeFi), enterprise applications, and institutions seeking real-world blockchain utility.

What sets Avalanche apart is its unique **consensus mechanism**, which blends aspects of classical consensus with Nakamoto consensus. This new model—called the **Avalanche consensus protocol**—allows the network to reach finality (transaction confirmation) in under 2 seconds, making it one of the fastest blockchains on the market. Transactions are confirmed nearly instantly, with extremely low fees, and the network can handle **thousands of transactions per second**.

Avalanche's architecture consists of **three interoperable blockchains**:

- The **X-Chain** (Exchange Chain): for creating and

transferring digital assets.

- The **P-Chain** (Platform Chain): for managing validators and coordinating custom blockchains.
- The **C-Chain** (Contract Chain): fully compatible with the Ethereum Virtual Machine (EVM), allowing developers to easily port over existing Ethereum smart contracts.

This **triple-chain structure** allows Avalanche to scale without congestion, maintain low transaction fees, and support a wide range of applications—from NFT marketplaces and games to financial instruments and custom enterprise solutions.

The native token of Avalanche is **AVAX**, used for transaction fees, staking, and governance. AVAX holders can delegate their tokens to validators and earn rewards while contributing to the network's security. With a capped supply and deflationary fee-burning mechanism, AVAX also has strong tokenomics that support long-term value.

Avalanche has positioned itself as a leader in **DeFi**, hosting major protocols such as Aave, Curve, Trader Joe, and Benqi. By offering Ethereum compatibility with higher performance and lower fees, it has attracted developers and liquidity away from Ethereum Layer 1. In fact, Avalanche has become a preferred network for users who want fast and cost-effective alternatives without leaving the familiar EVM environment.

In addition to its DeFi ecosystem, Avalanche supports **custom subnets**—dedicated blockchain networks that operate under the broader Avalanche consensus while having their own rules, tokenomics, and use cases. Subnets are ideal for enterprises and institutions that require compliance, privacy, or tailored performance. For example, **Deloitte** chose Avalanche to help improve FEMA's disaster relief processes. This kind of enterprise adoption highlights Avalanche's potential beyond retail crypto speculation.

Avalanche also supports **institutional-grade tokenization**, working on projects related to real-world assets such as real estate, equities, and debt instruments. Its focus on regulatory compliance, high throughput, and customizable infrastructure makes it well-suited for the coming wave of institutional blockchain integration.

Governance is a key feature of Avalanche's long-term vision. AVAX holders participate in on-chain governance by voting on upgrades, parameters, and development funding. This ensures that the community has direct influence over the network's direction and evolution.

Despite its rapid growth, Avalanche has had to navigate challenges—most notably during broader crypto market downturns and when competing chains introduced aggressive incentive programs. Still, it has maintained a strong development pace, user base, and reputation for reliability.

In summary, Avalanche is a powerful, fast, and flexible blockchain platform that serves a wide range of users—from retail DeFi participants to large-scale enterprises. With a unique architecture, innovative consensus protocol, and a growing list of real-world integrations, Avalanche is poised to be a key player in the **next phase of blockchain adoption**—where speed, customization, and regulatory readiness become critical factors for success.

Sophie's amazing discovery of Avalanche

Sophie was a fintech consultant in Frankfurt who had grown tired of the broken promise of speed in traditional finance. Wire transfers took days. Clearinghouses delayed settlements. Even so-called "instant" apps routed through layers of fees and approvals. But when she discovered DeFi, a new world opened up—one where finance could be fast, global, and programmable.

Her journey started on Ethereum, where she explored decentralized lending and yield farming. But congestion and high gas fees made it frustrating. Every transaction felt like squeezing through a bottleneck. She needed something faster, more scalable—without leaving the smart contract world she loved.

That's when she stumbled upon **Avalanche**.

The first time she used the **C-Chain**, she was amazed. A transaction that took minutes on Ethereum was confirmed in **less than two seconds**—for just pennies. She dove into Avalanche's architecture and found a system built for scale: a **three-chain structure**, subnets, and a consensus mechanism that rewrote the rules of speed and finality.

She quickly moved her liquidity operations to **Trader Joe**, Avalanche's leading DEX, and began optimizing yield strategies across **Benqi** and **Aave**. Returns were faster. Execution was smoother. Her clients noticed—and so did her competitors.

But Sophie didn't just want to optimize DeFi; she wanted to **bridge it with the real world**.

She pitched an idea to a mid-sized German bank: tokenized real estate investments on Avalanche. Traditional REITs were rigid, gated, and outdated. Avalanche's **subnet model** allowed her to build a custom blockchain—private, compliant, and fast—while still benefiting from Avalanche's security and infrastructure.

The bank was hesitant. Regulation. Risk. Unfamiliar territory. But Sophie demonstrated how the **P-Chain** could manage validator nodes with strict KYC, and how transactions on the subnet could settle instantly. Her proposal passed. The project launched.

Within six months, retail investors across Europe were buying tokenized shares in solar-powered housing projects. Instant ownership, automated dividends, and no need for paper trails. All powered by Avalanche.

Then came the phone call.

Deloitte wanted to collaborate. They had selected Avalanche for a government initiative involving disaster relief fund tracking. Sophie was stunned. It was validation—not just for her project, but for Avalanche's **enterprise-grade potential**.

She began hosting webinars and workshops, helping traditional firms onboard to Web3 using Avalanche subnets. Insurance companies. Logistics firms. Even public sector agencies. Each saw the same thing: speed, customization, and control.

But her favorite moment came during a developer event in Lisbon.

A group of high school students presented a game where in-game assets were NFTs minted on Avalanche. It used a subnet Sophie had helped design. Their project wasn't about finance—it was about freedom to build. And they were building fast.

That night, Sophie walked the cobbled streets of Lisbon with a smile. Avalanche wasn't just a blockchain. It was **infrastructure**—as fast as her ideas, as flexible as her ambition, and ready for the real world.

In a space filled with experiments and hype, Avalanche felt like a platform built for execution.

And Sophie? She was just getting started.

Chapter 8: Polygon — Scaling Ethereum Without Sacrificing Security

Ethereum has established itself as the most widely used platform for decentralized applications, but it suffers from scalability and high transaction fees. As adoption grew, the Ethereum network became congested, with users paying hundreds of dollars in gas fees for basic transactions. That's where **Polygon** stepped in—with a mission to scale Ethereum without compromising security, decentralization, or developer compatibility.

Polygon, originally called **Matic Network**, launched in 2017 and rebranded in 2021 to reflect its broader ambitions as a **scaling solution** for Ethereum. Rather than replacing Ethereum, Polygon enhances it by providing **Layer 2 solutions**—blockchains that operate alongside Ethereum to handle transactions more efficiently and at a lower cost.

The core idea behind Polygon is modular scalability. It offers a **suite of protocols** including sidechains, rollups (zk-Rollups and optimistic rollups), and enterprise-level chains, all built with Ethereum compatibility in mind. Developers can choose the scalability model that best fits their project's needs. The most well-known implementation is the **Polygon PoS Chain**, a sidechain that achieves consensus through a Proof-of-Stake system and is secured by validators staking **MATIC**, the network's native token.

The Polygon PoS Chain is **fully EVM-compatible**, meaning developers can deploy existing Ethereum smart contracts with zero modifications. This made it a hotbed for DeFi and NFT projects that wanted to keep Ethereum's security and ecosystem while improving user experience. Platforms like Aave, SushiSwap, and OpenSea have integrated with Polygon to offer faster, cheaper access to their services.

The real innovation came when Polygon expanded beyond PoS and launched **Polygon Supernets**, **Polygon Edge**, and most notably, **Polygon zkEVM**—a zero-knowledge scaling solution. **zkEVM** allows developers to execute Ethereum smart contracts on a high-speed Layer 2 chain while preserving cryptographic integrity and security. zk-Rollups bundle hundreds of transactions and publish a single cryptographic proof to Ethereum, reducing fees and congestion without compromising data validity.

Polygon also stands out in terms of **partnerships and real-world adoption**. The network has collaborated with major corporations like **Meta (Facebook)** for Instagram's NFT integration, **Nike** for digital collectibles, and **Starbucks** for loyalty reward systems. These high-profile use cases demonstrate Polygon's potential to bridge mainstream and blockchain technology.

The native token **MATIC** serves multiple roles: it pays for gas fees on Polygon chains, is staked to secure the network, and is used for governance as Polygon moves toward decentralized protocol management. The token has a fixed supply and undergoes periodic burns, contributing to its long-term value potential.

Polygon's developer tools and ecosystem funding are robust. The team has launched multiple grant programs, hackathons, and accelerator initiatives to onboard new developers and encourage innovation. With a strong community and developer-first approach, Polygon has attracted thousands of projects and millions of users.

Security is a top priority for Polygon. While sidechains inherently carry more risk than Layer 1 blockchains, the Polygon team conducts extensive audits and collaborates with security firms to minimize vulnerabilities. The launch of **Polygon Avail**, a data availability layer, aims to further improve the security and resilience of off-chain data storage and validation.

In short, Polygon is one of the most pragmatic, flexible, and enterprise-friendly solutions in the crypto space. Instead of competing with Ethereum, it complements it—giving users and developers an efficient way to access the Ethereum ecosystem at scale. As demand for blockchain-based apps continues to rise, Polygon is uniquely positioned to absorb that growth and help Ethereum become truly global infrastructure.

Polygon and Nina

Nina was a UX designer based in Mumbai. She wasn't a developer or a crypto expert, but she had a mission: to make decentralized apps feel as seamless and intuitive as traditional platforms. She believed that blockchain wasn't just for techies—it was for everyone. But the first time she tried to mint an NFT on Ethereum, the experience was painful. The gas fee was higher than the artwork. The transaction took ages. And the wallet interface made her feel like she was coding just to buy a picture.

Frustrated, she began searching for something better.

That's when she found **Polygon**.

Polygon felt like Ethereum—but smoother, faster, cheaper. She minted her next NFT for less than a rupee. It confirmed almost instantly. And everything still worked inside MetaMask, just like before. She was hooked.

She dove into the community and discovered how Polygon

wasn't a competitor to Ethereum—it was an ally. A **Layer 2** chain designed to scale Ethereum's reach without sacrificing its values. She learned about the **Polygon PoS Chain**, the **zkEVM**, and even **Polygon Edge**, which let people build their own blockchain ecosystems with Ethereum compatibility.

Her mind raced with ideas.

She sketched a platform that could help Indian musicians tokenize their songs, share royalties instantly, and give fans ownership in their success—all on Polygon. She called it **BeatChain**. Within a month, she teamed up with a developer and launched the MVP. Artists uploaded their tracks. Smart contracts split royalties. Fans bought limited-edition music NFTs that gave them backstage access and merch discounts.

Because it ran on Polygon, every interaction was cheap and fast. Users didn't complain about fees or wait times. They just... used it. Like any other app.

BeatChain caught fire in India's indie music scene. Soon, artists in Mumbai, Bangalore, and even small towns were using it. A song from a street performer in Pune sold out its first collection of 100 NFTs in hours. The money went straight to her wallet, and the fans proudly shared their NFT badges on social media.

Then came the Meta partnership.

Instagram announced it would support NFT minting and sharing through **Polygon**. Nina couldn't believe it. Suddenly, her platform was aligned with the biggest social media app in the world. She integrated a sharing feature, and users could now display their BeatChain collectibles directly on their Instagram profiles.

Investors came knocking. But Nina stayed true to her mission. She launched a **Supernet**—a dedicated Polygon chain for BeatChain alone, giving her full control over governance, fees, and upgrades. It was her own digital city built on a foundation of Ethereum-compatible infrastructure.

She attended a Polygon conference in Dubai, where she met builders from Nike, Starbucks, and Reddit—each integrating Polygon for loyalty rewards, digital merch, and community experiences. What united them all was the belief that **blockchain should be invisible**. The user shouldn't feel the friction. They should feel the freedom.

By year two, BeatChain had onboarded over 200,000 users. Many had never touched crypto before. For them, Polygon wasn't a "Layer 2." It was just what made things *work*.

One night, Nina sat on her balcony, the sounds of music

drifting from a local bar down the street. She opened her laptop and browsed through the latest stats—10,000 NFTs minted this week, 92% user retention, zero user complaints about gas fees.

Polygon had made it possible.

It didn't promise the moon. It promised something better: usability, speed, and affordability.

And in Nina's hands, that was enough to **change an industry**.

Chapter 9: Ripple (XRP) – The Bridge Between Traditional Finance and Crypto

While most cryptocurrencies focus on disrupting traditional finance, **Ripple** takes a different approach–it seeks to integrate with it. Ripple's primary goal is to create a **real-time global settlement network** that enables instant, low-cost, and cross-border payments for banks, financial institutions, and remittance providers. The digital asset at the center of this ecosystem is **XRP**.

Founded in 2012, Ripple Labs created the **RippleNet** platform, which enables institutions to settle cross-border transactions in real-time, with end-to-end transparency and minimal fees. Unlike Bitcoin and Ethereum, which rely on mining, Ripple's XRP Ledger uses a **unique consensus protocol** that's faster, more energy-efficient, and can handle 1,500 transactions per second with settlement times under five seconds.

RippleNet offers several products–**xCurrent**, **xVia**, and **On-Demand Liquidity (ODL)**. ODL is where XRP plays a critical role. Traditionally, sending money from one country to another requires multiple intermediaries, including banks, currency exchanges, and clearing houses–resulting in delays and high fees. With ODL, institutions can use XRP as a **bridge**

currency between fiat pairs. For example, dollars can be converted to XRP in one country, sent across the XRP Ledger, and instantly converted to pesos on the other side. This eliminates the need for pre-funded accounts in foreign countries.

XRP's speed, liquidity, and low cost make it an ideal intermediary asset. Unlike stablecoins, XRP is not backed by fiat reserves; it is independent, decentralized, and traded on global markets. Its fixed supply of 100 billion tokens—many of which are held in escrow by Ripple Labs—has been both a strength and a source of criticism. Supporters appreciate the transparent escrow mechanism that releases XRP into circulation on a predictable schedule, while critics argue the company holds too much influence.

Despite controversy, Ripple has achieved significant adoption. Over 300 financial institutions in more than 40 countries have signed up for RippleNet services. These include major players such as Santander, SBI Holdings, and American Express. Ripple's focus on compliance and regulatory cooperation has made it attractive to institutions wary of other crypto networks.

However, Ripple's journey hasn't been without turbulence. In 2020, the **U.S. Securities and Exchange Commission**

(SEC) filed a lawsuit alleging that Ripple Labs conducted an unregistered securities offering by selling XRP. The legal battle caused many exchanges to delist XRP and created long-term uncertainty. Yet, in 2023, Ripple secured a partial legal victory when a judge ruled that XRP sales on secondary markets did not constitute securities—revitalizing interest in the project and restoring listings on several platforms.

XRP's use case extends beyond payments. The XRP Ledger supports **tokenization of real-world assets**, **decentralized exchange (DEX) functionality**, and **smart contracts** through its native scripting language. Its energy efficiency and throughput make it suitable for central bank digital currencies (CBDCs), which Ripple is actively developing with various national governments.

The Ripple team is also expanding into enterprise blockchain services, including solutions for trade finance, identity, and compliance. The **Ripple CBDC Platform**, launched in 2023, enables governments and banks to issue digital currencies on private versions of the XRP Ledger with full control and interoperability.

In conclusion, Ripple and XRP represent a different kind of cryptocurrency philosophy: one that **partners with traditional finance** instead of replacing it. With real-world adoption, regulatory resilience, and strong infrastructure for global payments, XRP continues to play a unique and important role in the evolution of digital finance. For investors looking at utility, institutional adoption, and infrastructure-focused projects, XRP deserves serious consideration.

How Emilio discovered XRP

Emilio worked at a remittance kiosk in Manila, where families lined up for hours to receive money sent from relatives abroad. The process was slow and frustrating. People waited in long queues, paid high fees, and sometimes had to return the next day when banks delayed the release of funds. Emilio had worked there for five years, and every day he asked himself the same question: *Why does sending money still feel like mailing a letter in 1995?*

Then one day, a customer mentioned **Ripple**.

"Do you accept XRP?" the young man asked.

Emilio had heard of Bitcoin, but not XRP. That night, he searched online and learned that Ripple wasn't just another cryptocurrency. It was a system designed to help banks and remittance companies **move money instantly across**

borders. XRP wasn't trying to replace the banks—it was **helping them evolve**.

What fascinated him most was Ripple's concept of **On-Demand Liquidity (ODL)**. Instead of pre-funding accounts in multiple countries, institutions could use XRP as a bridge currency. Dollars could be instantly converted to XRP, sent to another country, and converted to pesos—all within seconds. It cut out the delays. It cut out the intermediaries.

Emilio was inspired.

He approached his supervisor with a bold idea: run a pilot program using XRP for cross-border transfers. It would start with one corridor—U.S. to the Philippines. At first, the management was skeptical, but Emilio presented a clear plan, citing Ripple's partnerships with banks and the network's **regulatory focus**. He showed how XRP transactions were **fast, cheap, and traceable**.

They agreed to test it.

Within a week of integrating RippleNet, they saw results. What once took two to three days now took **under ten seconds**. Transfer fees dropped by over 70%. And for Emilio, the best moment came when a grandmother in Cebu City smiled and said, “My son sent this money an hour ago. I’ve never received it so fast.”

The pilot expanded. More currencies. More corridors. Eventually, Emilio’s kiosk became the first in his region to fully integrate Ripple for remittances. Customers came from miles away just to avoid the delays and costs of legacy systems.

But it wasn’t all smooth.

When the **SEC lawsuit** against Ripple hit the news, Emilio feared the worst. Was it over? Would the kiosk have to shut down the program? But he followed the case closely, read updates, and watched as Ripple **fought back**. Then came the partial victory in court—the ruling that secondary market sales of XRP were not securities. Exchanges re-listed XRP. Confidence returned.

Emilio saw this as proof: **Ripple wasn’t going anywhere**.

He began educating customers and colleagues about XRP. He hosted workshops, joined webinars, and even launched a YouTube channel explaining Ripple in local dialects. One of his videos—“XRP for OFWs” (Overseas Filipino Workers)—went viral.

He earned the nickname *Mr. XRP* in his city.

One year later, Emilio was invited to speak at a fintech summit in Singapore. There, he met Ripple executives and told them how their protocol had transformed lives in his community. They listened. They asked questions. They thanked him.

On the flight home, Emilio reflected. Ripple hadn't just sped up remittances. It had **empowered him to lead**. To bridge the gap between old and new. Between finance and the people who depend on it every day.

And for every second shaved off a transaction time... for every peso saved on a remittance fee... he knew XRP was doing what it was meant to do.

Chapter 10: Litecoin — Digital Silver for Everyday Payments

Often referred to as the **"digital silver"** to Bitcoin's gold, **Litecoin (LTC)** is one of the oldest and most consistently active cryptocurrencies in existence. Launched in 2011 by **Charlie Lee**, a former Google engineer and ex-Director of Engineering at Coinbase, Litecoin was designed to improve upon Bitcoin's limitations, particularly in terms of transaction speed and scalability.

Litecoin shares many similarities with Bitcoin but offers **faster transaction times** and **lower fees**, making it better suited for day-to-day payments. Where Bitcoin blocks are mined every 10 minutes, Litecoin cuts that time down to **2.5 minutes**, enabling quicker confirmation and usability in retail and online commerce settings. Its average transaction cost is just a few cents, regardless of the transfer size—an attractive feature for microtransactions and international remittances.

Technically, Litecoin is a **Proof-of-Work (PoW)** cryptocurrency like Bitcoin, but it uses a different hashing algorithm called **Scrypt**. This algorithm is more memory-intensive and was originally developed to democratize mining and reduce the advantage of specialized ASIC hardware. Although ASICs eventually became common for Scrypt as well, the Scrypt algorithm helped decentralize Litecoin's mining base in its early years.

The total supply of LTC is **84 million coins**—four times Bitcoin's 21 million. This larger supply means that individual coin units are cheaper in price, even if market cap remains significantly lower than Bitcoin's. Litecoin also undergoes **halving events** every four years, reducing the block reward given to miners. These halvings create scarcity and can lead to price appreciation due to reduced new supply.

Litecoin is often referred to as a **testbed for Bitcoin** because it implements new features and upgrades earlier than Bitcoin. For instance, it was one of the first major cryptocurrencies to adopt **Segregated Witness (SegWit)**, which improves transaction efficiency and scalability. Litecoin also successfully activated **Lightning Network** transactions—instant, low-cost, off-chain transactions that are ideal for retail payments.

One of the most innovative upgrades to Litecoin is **MimbleWimble via Extension Blocks (MWEB)**. Introduced in 2022, this privacy-focused feature allows users to send confidential transactions that hide transaction amounts while remaining secure and verifiable. MWEB enhances fungibility and user privacy without turning Litecoin into a fully anonymous coin, striking a regulatory-friendly balance.

Litecoin has built a reputation for reliability. Over a decade after launch, it has **never gone offline**, suffered major exploits, or been significantly censored. This stability is part of what has kept Litecoin in the top tier of cryptocurrencies in terms of both market capitalization and real-world utility. It's listed on virtually every crypto exchange, supported by most wallets, and accepted by thousands of merchants globally.

While Litecoin lacks the flashy narratives of DeFi, NFTs, or Web3 platforms, its simplicity is its strength. It's easy to understand, easy to use, and has an established role as a **medium of exchange** in the crypto ecosystem. For users who want a cryptocurrency they can use for actual spending—not just holding—Litecoin delivers.

LTC is often used in **remittances**, **point-of-sale systems**, and **cross-border payments**, especially in regions where traditional banking infrastructure is unreliable. Its fast confirmation time and low fees make it ideal for developing economies where transaction costs matter significantly more than high-throughput smart contract capabilities.

In conclusion, Litecoin may not be the future of decentralized applications or programmable finance, but it plays a crucial and consistent role in the crypto economy. It represents the **digital cash layer** of the cryptocurrency stack—secure, efficient, and battle-tested. For users, investors, and merchants seeking a dependable digital currency for daily transactions, Litecoin remains one of the most practical and trusted options in the space.

Jake, the barista

Jake was a barista in a small Colorado town with a big problem—every time he tried to send money to his cousin in Guatemala, the process was slow and expensive. The wire transfer took three days, the fees were outrageous, and sometimes the money got stuck in the system for no clear reason. All he wanted was a way to send $50 that would actually *arrive* quickly and intact.

One afternoon, a customer wearing a hoodie with a Litecoin logo noticed Jake staring at his phone in frustration. "Ever try crypto?" he asked casually. "Litecoin's good for that."

Jake shrugged. "I've heard of Bitcoin."

"Too slow. Too expensive," the man said. "Litecoin's faster. Cheaper. Built for payments."

Jake was skeptical but curious. That night, he downloaded a Litecoin wallet and spent $20 on LTC. The next day, he sent it to his cousin in Guatemala, who had just learned about crypto through a local merchant that accepted it for groceries.

The transaction arrived in under a minute. The fee? Less than one cent.

Jake was blown away.

He started using Litecoin more—first for remittances, then for paying freelance artists online, then even to tip musicians at his local open mic night. The speed, simplicity, and low cost made it feel like cash in the digital world.

Soon, he convinced his boss to start accepting Litecoin at the café. They placed a small QR code on the counter. At first, it was just curious customers, but then more and more people started paying with LTC—especially travelers and digital nomads who didn't want to use cards or cash. It turned into a talking point. A vibe.

Jake began reading about Litecoin's history. He admired how it had been running for over a decade with zero downtime. It didn't try to be flashy. No promises of world domination. Just reliable digital money. He liked that.

He followed the community updates and saw how Litecoin had implemented **MimbleWimble** for privacy. Not everyone needed it, but it was good to know there was an option to keep your financial life from becoming public record. He also loved how Litecoin embraced upgrades like **SegWit** and the **Lightning Network**. It reminded him of an old pickup truck that had been tuned to race like a sports car.

At one point, Jake started using the Lightning Network for instant micropayments. He paid a podcast creator in Norway 10 cents per episode. It felt revolutionary—supporting creators directly, globally, instantly.

He wrote a blog post about his experience. It got picked up by a crypto newsletter. Then, someone invited him to speak at a Litecoin community event in Austin. Jake was nervous, but he went.

He stood in front of developers, miners, and merchants and told them what Litecoin meant to him—not as a trader or techie, but as a guy who just wanted to help his cousin buy groceries in real time. He told them about the café, about the travelers, about the joy of sending and receiving value without asking anyone for permission.

When he finished, people clapped—not for the speech, but for the simplicity of it all.

Litecoin wasn't trending on Twitter. It wasn't making headlines every week. But it was **working**—quietly, efficiently, globally. And in that quiet, Jake found something rare: a technology that did exactly what it promised.

Epilogue: The Future of Cryptocurrency Is Diverse, Not Singular

As you reach the end of this book, one truth should be clear: there is **no single coin that defines the crypto space**. While Bitcoin may be the origin, and Ethereum may be the dominant platform, the reality is far more complex—and far more exciting.

You've now explored a range of cryptocurrencies, each with its own vision, utility, and community. **Bitcoin** stands as digital gold. **Ethereum** powers the smart contract revolution. **Solana** brings speed to the forefront. **Chainlink** connects blockchains to the real world. **Cardano** builds with academic rigor. **Polkadot** unites fragmented ecosystems. **Avalanche** offers speed and enterprise customization. **Polygon** scales Ethereum's reach. **XRP** bridges the traditional and digital. And **Litecoin** remains a quiet champion of simplicity and usability.

The lesson here isn't just that these projects exist—it's that **they coexist**. We're witnessing a shift from a mono-chain mindset to a **multi-chain reality**. Just as the internet evolved from a few websites to billions of interconnected services, so too will the blockchain landscape expand—with each protocol serving unique purposes in a vast digital economy.

What you should walk away with isn't just technical understanding—it's strategic awareness. If you're an investor, this means building a portfolio that reflects the strengths of each ecosystem. If you're a builder, this means choosing the right chain based on your product's goals. And if you're a curious learner, this means recognizing that innovation doesn't always come from the most popular project—it often comes from the one solving a problem no one else dared to touch.

It's also important to understand the role of **regulation** in the years ahead. Governments are no longer ignoring crypto—they're engaging with it, cautiously and sometimes aggressively. Coins like XRP, which fought regulatory battles, have emerged with greater clarity and resilience. Others, like Cardano, have built with regulation in mind from the start. As blockchain goes mainstream, regulatory frameworks will shape winners and losers.

Meanwhile, **emerging markets** are adopting crypto not as a novelty—but as necessity. From remittances in Southeast Asia to NFTs in Africa to tokenized finance in Latin America, we're seeing real-world impact far from Silicon Valley. This isn't just a digital movement—it's a **global economic revolution**.

Technology is evolving fast. Zero-knowledge proofs, account abstraction, cross-chain messaging, decentralized identity, and AI-integrated finance are already reshaping the road ahead. Staying informed and adaptable will be essential.

So what's next?

That's up to you.

Whether you're here to invest, build, teach, or explore, you now hold a deeper understanding of the top cryptocurrencies shaping our digital future. Use this knowledge. Share it. Apply it. Question it.

Because crypto isn't about speculation. It's about **sovereignty**, **efficiency**, **inclusion**, and **freedom**. And the more you understand the technologies powering this movement, the more equipped you'll be to take advantage of the opportunity that still lies ahead.

Thank you for listening—and welcome to the future of finance.

www.ingramcontent.com/pod-product-compliance
Lightning Source LLC
LaVergne TN
LVHW022024200926
848481LV00007B/2526